Signing in My World

SIGN LANGUAGE FOR KIDS

by Kathryn Clay

illustrated by Daniel Griffo

Consultant: Kari Sween
Adjunct Instructor of
American Sign Language
Minnesota State University, Mankato

56128283

CAPSTONE PRESS
a capstone imprint

TABLE OF CONTENTS

How to Use This Guide

This book is full of useful words in both English and American Sign Language (ASL). The English word and sign for each word appear next to the picture. Arrows are used to show movement for some signs.

Most ASL signs are understood wherever you go. But some signs may change depending on where you are. It's like having a different accent.

For example, New Yorkers sign "pizza" like this:

People in other places might sign "pizza" like this:

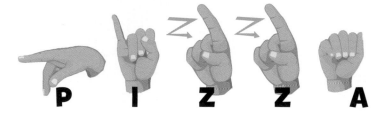

or this:

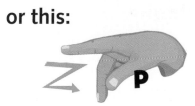

People will not understand you if they can't see your signs. Make sure your hands are always in view when signing with someone. Don't be afraid to ask people to slow down or sign again if you don't understand a sign.

Brief Introduction to American Sign Language (ASL)

Many people who are deaf or hard of hearing use ASL to talk. Hearing people may also learn ASL to communicate with deaf friends and family members.

Signs can be very different from one another. Signs may use one or both hands. Sometimes signs have more than one step. For other signs, you must move your entire body. If there is no sign for a word, you can fingerspell it.

People use facial expressions when they sign. They smile when signing good news. They frown when signing sad news. Body language is also important. Someone might sign slowly to show that he or she is very tired.

It's important to remember that learning to sign is like learning any language. ASL becomes easier with practice and patience.

Alphabet Chart

ASL has a sign for every letter of the English alphabet. If there is no sign for a word, you can use letter signs to spell out the word. Fingerspelling is often used to sign the names of people and places.

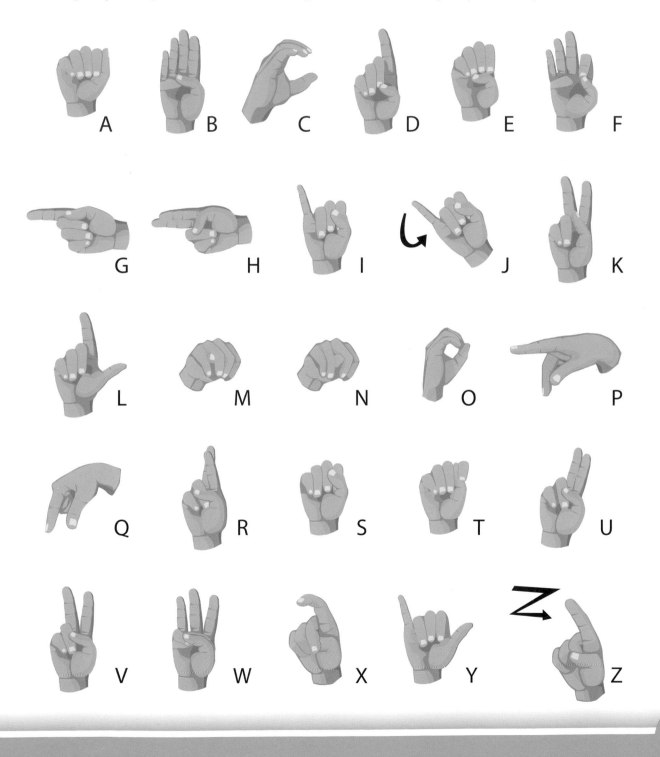

PEOPLE

Make P shapes and move hands in circles.

man Bring thumb to chest.

woman Bring thumb to chest.

baby Move arms as if rocking a baby.

boy Close hand while moving it away from forehead.

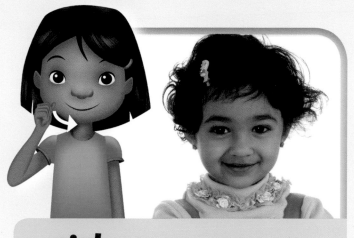

girl Slide thumb down cheek.

you Point to person.

me Point to self.

BODY

Slide hands down chest.

eyes Point to each eye.

head Bring hand to chin.

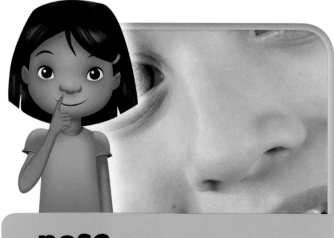

nose Tap nose twice.

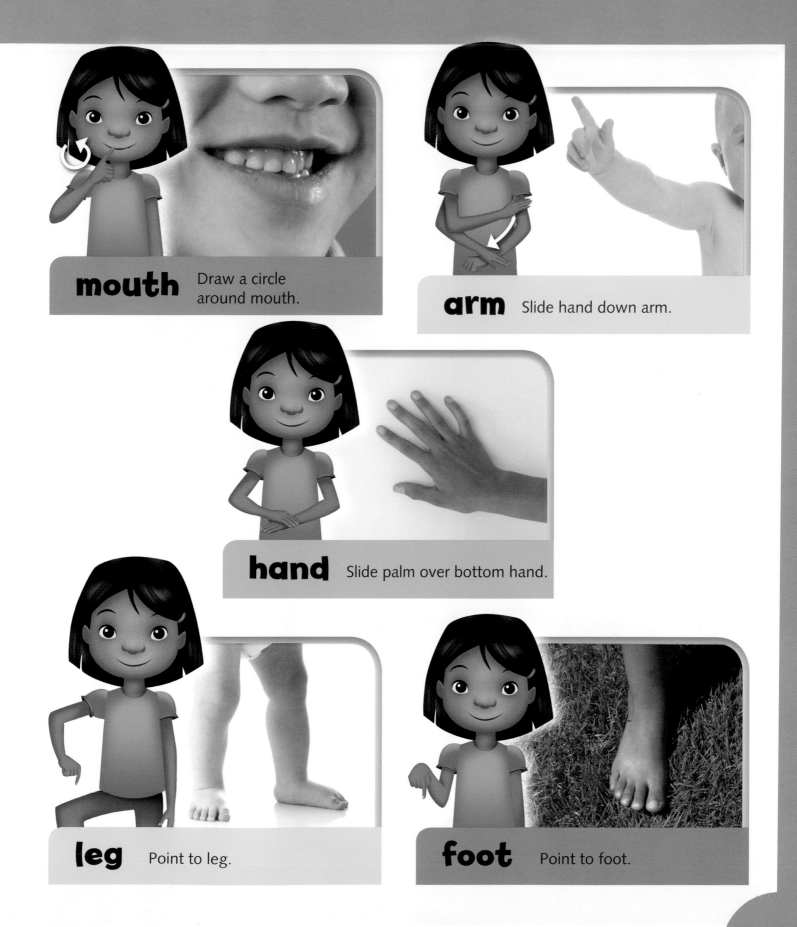

mouth Draw a circle around mouth.

arm Slide hand down arm.

hand Slide palm over bottom hand.

leg Point to leg.

foot Point to foot.

GREETINGS

Move hand away from forehead.

hello Wave hand.

good-bye Open and close hand.

My name is _____

1. Palm to chest. 2. Bring fingers together. 3. Fingerspell name.

What's your name?

1. Point to person. 2. Bring fingers together. 3. Move hands in small circles.

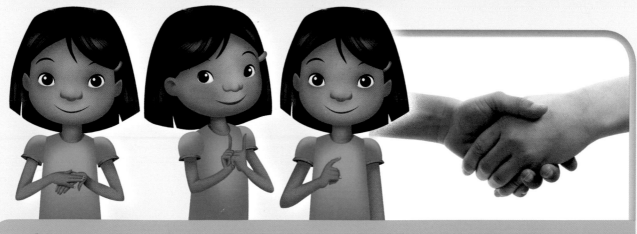

Nice to meet you

1. Slide palm across other palm. 2. Bring wrists together. 3. Point to person.

CONVERSATION

Make C shapes and move hands back and forth.

yes Make a fist. Move hand up and down.

no Bring fingers together.

maybe
1. Raise one hand while lowering the other.
2. Move hands back and forth.

more Bring fingers together.

now Make Y shapes and bring hands down.

later Make L shape and move wrist forward.

Combine the shapes I, L, and Y.

or

I love you 1. Point to self. 2. Cross wrists. 3. Point to person.

OPPOSITES

Move fingers apart.

big Make L shapes and move hands apart.

small Bring hands close together.

good Move hand away from mouth.

bad Move hand away from mouth while turning palm down.

new Slide back of hand over palm.

old Close fist while moving hand down.

fast Bend fingers as you move hands up.

slow Slide hand up along arm.

hot Make C shape and move hand away from mouth and down.

cold Shake fists as if shivering.

QUESTIONS

Draw a question mark with finger.

who Touch thumb to chin and wiggle index finger

what Shake hands slightly.

when Circle index finger around other finger.

where Wiggle finger twice.

why
1. Touch fingers to forehead.
2. Bring hand down and make Y shape.

how much Open hand with palm facing up.

how many Open hands with palms facing up.

FEELINGS

Move middle finger up chest.

sad Move hands down in front of face.

happy Make two small circles at chest.

scared Make fists and open hands with palms facing chest.

angry Bend fingers and bring toward face.

surprised Make fists and point index fingers.

excited Bend middle fingers and make small circles at chest.

tired Bend wrists down.

bored Twist finger at side of nose.

MANNERS

Touch chest twice with thumb.

please Make a circle on chest.

thank you Move hand away from lips.

20

excuse me
Slide fingers along palm.

congratulations
Clasp hands together and shake twice.

I'm sorry
Make a fist and move hand in a circle.

SEASONS

1. Make S shape.
2. Move fist in a circle against palm.

rain Move hands down.

spring Move hand up and through other hand twice.

autumn
Move hand past elbow twice, like a leaf falling from a tree.

winter
Shake fists as if shivering.

snow
Wiggle fingers while bringing hands down.

summer
Bend finger while sliding across forehead.

BIRTHDAY

Bring middle finger from chin to chest.

friend 1. Lock fingers. 2. Repeat with other hand on top.

balloon Move hands into a circle, like blowing up a balloon.

candy Twist finger on cheek.

candles Wiggle fingers and point to wrist.

ice cream Make S shape and move down twice in front of mouth.

gift Make X shapes and move forward twice.

cake Make C shape and slide down hand.

HOLIDAYS

Tap chest twice.

New Year's Day

1. Slide back of hand over palm.
2. Make S shape. Move top hand in a circle.
3. Bring arm down to other arm.

Valentine's Day

1. Make a heart shape on chest.
2. Bring arm down to other arm.

Halloween

Cover face and then open hands, like playing peek-a-boo.

Thanksgiving

Move hands away from mouth with a small bounce.

Christmas

Make C shape and move across chest.

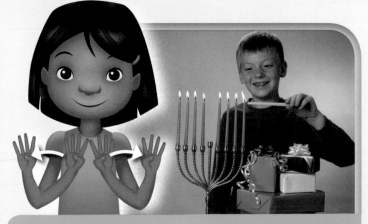

Hanukkah

Hold up four fingers. Slide hands to the side.

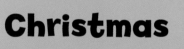

27

SPECIAL EVENTS

1. Grab finger and pull up.
2. Bend middle fingers.
   Curve up and out.

party   Make P shapes and twist wrists.

celebration   Make X shapes and move wrists in small circles

wedding Grab fingers with other hand.

carnival Bend fingers and move in circles.

circus Close fingers and wiggle hand in front of nose.

applause Twist hands near face.

29

GLOSSARY

accent—the way people say words differently based on where they live

body language—the act of sharing information by using gestures, movements, and facial expressions

communicate—to share thoughts, feelings, or information

deaf—unable to hear

facial expression—feelings shared by making different faces; making an angry face to show you are mad, for example

BOOKS IN THIS SERIES

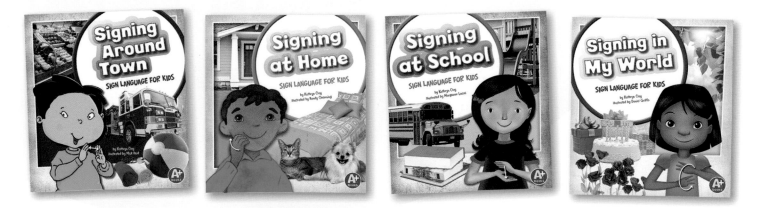

READ MORE

Nelson, Michiyo. *Sign Language: My First 100 Words.*
New York: Scholastic, 2008.

Petelinsek, Kathleen, and E. Russell Primm.
Greetings and Phrases. Talking Hands.
Chanhassen, Minn.: The Child's World, 2006.

Schaefer, Lola M. *Some Kids Are Deaf.*
Mankato, Minn.: Capstone Press, 2008.

INTERNET SITES

FactHound offers a safe, fun way to find Internet sites related to this book. All of the sites on FactHound have been researched by our staff.

Here's all you do:

Visit *www.facthound.com*

Type in this code: 9781620650547

 Super-cool stuff! Check out projects, games and lots more at **www.capstonekids.com**

A+ Books are published by Capstone Press,
1710 Roe Crest Drive, North Mankato, Minnesota 56003
www.capstonepub.com

Library of Congress Cataloging-in-Publication Data
Clay, Kathryn.
 Signing in my world : sign language for kids / by Kathryn Clay.
  pages cm.—(A+ books. Time to sign)
 Summary: "Illustrations of American Sign Language, along with labeled photos,
introduce children to words and phrases for feelings, holidays, manners, body parts,
and more"—Provided by publisher.
 ISBN 978-1-62065-054-7 (library binding)
 ISBN 978-1-4765-3359-9 (ebook PDF)
 1. American Sign Language—Juvenile literature. 2. English language—Alphabet—
Juvenile literature. I. Title.
HV2480.C54 2014
372.6—dc23   2013010642

Editorial Credits
Tracy Davies McCabe, designer; Svetlana Zhurkin, media researcher;
Kathy McColley, production specialist

Photo Credits
Capstone Studio: Karon Dubke, 8, 9 (top left, middle, and bottom right), 18 (top left and top right), 19 (top left and
bottom right), 23 (top right), 24, 25, 26 (bottom), 27 (bottom right), 28 (top), 29 (middle right); iStockphotos: Bastun,
3, 5, Carmen Martínez Banús, 29 (bottom), Peter Topp Engelsted Jonasen, 29 (middle left); Shutterstock: Alex
Staroseltsev, 15 (bottom right), Aliaksei Hintau, cover (middle left), Ami Parikh, 7 (right), ampyang, 10 (bottom),
Andrea Slatter, 19 (middle), Andy Dean Photography, 7 (left), Anneka, 14 (bottom right), 16 (bottom), auremar, 28
(bottom), bikeriderlondon, 21 (middle), Brian Chase, 27 (middle), Bronwyn Photo, 21 (top), CandyBox Images,
20 (bottom), Cheryl E. Davis, 27 (bottom left), Creativa, 17 (bottom), Daboost, 15 (top right), Dayna More, 16
(top), G. K., 22 (top), gillmar, 23 (top left), glayan, 6 (bottom), Ilike, 15 (top left), Janina Dierks, 26 (top), Jeff
Thrower, 6 (middle), Jeka, 19 (bottom left), Juriah Mosin, 19 (top right), 20 (top), merzzie, 6 (top), Morgan
Lane Photography, 27 (top), mypokcik, 22 (bottom), Nagel Photography, 10 (top), Natalia Siverina, 17
(middle left), Pakhnyushcha, 14 (top right), Piotr Marcinski, 9 (bottom left), Sandra van der Steen, 11,
scattoselvaggio, 15 (middle left), sebra, 18 (bottom), Sergey Khamidulin, 9 (top right), sianc, 17 (top),
Soon Wee Hong, 17 (middle right), spfotocz, 29 (top), Sunny Forest, 23 (bottom left), Susi, cover
(bottom left), Talvi, 14 (top left), Twin Design, 15 (middle right), Valeev, 15 (bottom left), Vitaly
Krivosheev, cover (top right), Wallenrock, 23 (bottom right), Yuri Arcurs, 14 (bottom left),
Zurijeta, 16 (middle), 21 (bottom)

Note to Parents, Teachers, and Librarians
This accessible, visual guide uses full color photographs and illustrations
and inviting content to introduce young readers to American Sign Language.
The book provides an early introduction to reference materials and encourages
further learning by including the following sections: Table of Contents,
Alphabet Chart, Glossary, Read More, and Internet Sites.

Printed in the United States of America in North Mankato, Minnesota.
022014   008009R